FROM THE HEART OF THE CARIBBEAN

The Landscape of St Lucia

g

ALISON BROWNLIE

THE PEOPLE OF ST LUCIA
THE LANDSCAPE OF ST LUCIA

Cover: A view of Gros Piton.
Title page: Local people enjoy the sun on one of St Lucia's many beautiful beaches.
Imprint page: Fishing boats lined up on the coast of Anse la Raye.

Designers: Jan Sterling Associates (cover) and Mark Whitchurch (insides)
Production controller: Carol Titchener

Picture Acknowledgements:
All photographs are by Jeremy Horner except St Lucia Tourist Board 26. All map artwork is by Peter Bull. Line artwork on the cover and repeated on the inside design is by Jan Sterling.

First published in 1998 by Wayland Publishers Limited
This paperback edition published in 2001 by
Hodder Wayland, an imprint of Hodder Children's Books

Updated & reprinted in 2004

The author wishes to thank Alison Corfield and Nigel File for providing additional information.

© Hodder Wayland 1998

British Library Cataloguing in Publication Data
Brownlie, Alison
 The landscape of St Lucia. – (From the heart of the Caribbean)
 1. Saint Lucia – Geography – Juvenile literature
 I. Title
 917.2'9843

ISBN 0 7502 3822 4

Typeset by Mark Whitchurch
Printed in China by
WKT Company Ltd

Contents

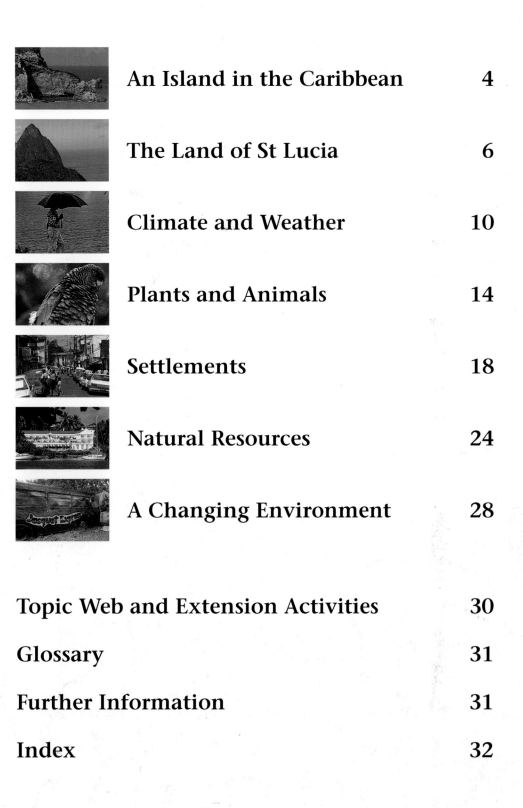

An Island in the Caribbean

Right in the heart of the Caribbean Sea lies a long chain of small, volcanic islands, called the Windward Islands. St Lucia is the second-largest island in this group and lies just south of Martinique and north of St Vincent. St Lucia is an island of many landscapes, from rain forest and mountains at its centre, to beautiful sandy beaches on its coast.

LANDSCAPE FACTS

Capital:	Castries
Area:	616 square kilometres
Highest point:	Mount Gimie (958 metres)
Longest river:	Cul de Sac River
Volcano:	Soufrière

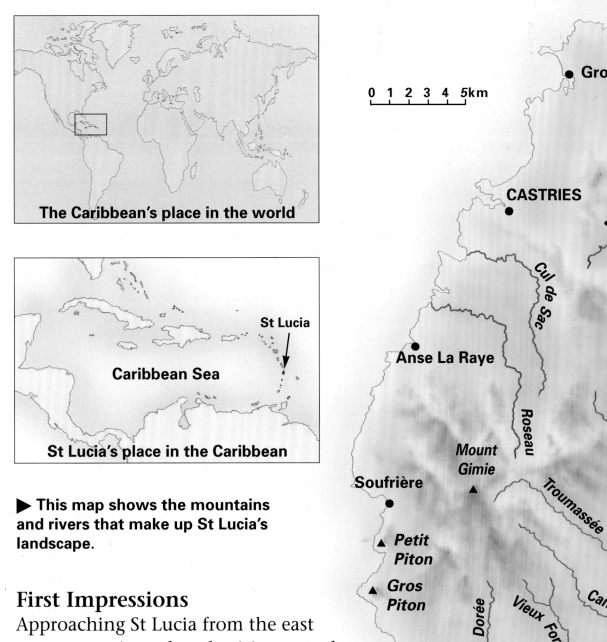

The Caribbean's place in the world

St Lucia

Caribbean Sea

St Lucia's place in the Caribbean

N

0 1 2 3 4 5km

Gros Islet

CASTRIES

Marquis

Cul de Sac

Dennery

Roseau

Anse La Raye

Mount Gimie

Troumassée

Soufrière

Petit Piton

Gros Piton

Dorée

Vieux Fort

Canelles

Vieux Fort

▶ This map shows the mountains and rivers that make up St Lucia's landscape.

First Impressions

Approaching St Lucia from the east you can see jagged peaks rising out of the water with high, limestone cliffs. Deep ravines separate the mountains and hills. The west coast is less rugged and it is here that you find splendid sandy beaches.

Where the land is less steep, around the coast and in broad river valleys, the land has been cleared of forest and farming takes place. But much of the island is too steep for this.

The Land of St Lucia

The centre of St Lucia is remote and difficult to get to. The steep hillsides of the central highlands are covered in dense rain forest. The soil is fertile here and supports a wide variety of tropical plants and flowers, such as hibiscus and bougainvillaea.

Dense rain forest ▶ grows in the centre of the island.

Rivers

St Lucia's eight main rivers start within a few kilometres of each other. They flow from the centre of the island like the spokes of a bicycle wheel, forming a 'radial' pattern. The rivers flow the short distance to the sea, through the rain forest, cutting deep ravines and valleys. Nearer the coast, the valleys flatten out. During storms and hurricanes these rivers can become raging torrents, strong enough to sweep away houses and bridges.

▰▰ CASE STUDY ▰▰

Cul de Sac River
Cul de Sac River begins its journey near the summit of Mount Gimie. It is the longest river on the island. It flows northwards, irrigating the large Cul de Sac banana plantation on its way as it bends to the west. The river finally meets the sea at Cul de Sac Bay, just south of Castries.

▲ **By the time the Cul de Sac River reaches the sea it is flowing more slowly and has broadened out.**

◀ **Diamond Falls, near Soufrière. Small waterfalls, such as this one, form where streams have eroded away the land.**

RAIN FOREST FACT
Only 10 per cent of St Lucia's
land is still rain forest.

▼ A view of Gros Piton, one of St Lucia's 'twin peaks'.

Twin Peaks

Volcanic activity produced the mountains of St Lucia. Over millions of years these mountains have been eroded by rivers. Although Mount Gimie is the highest mountain on the island, the twin peaks of Gros Piton and Petit Piton are more famous. They are old volcanic plugs, which rise dramatically straight out of the sea. For St Lucians the Pitons are an important symbol of their homeland. They are even represented on the national flag.

A Drive-in Volcano

Not far from Mount Gimie is Soufrière. This is the crater of an old volcano. The gas and steam from sulphur springs give off unpleasant smells. Pools of boiling water bubble away here, and the rocks are so hot you can cook an egg on them. People in St Lucia claim that this is the only 'drive-in volcano' in the world. In spite of the splutterings of Soufrière, there has not been any serious volcanic activity here since 1766.

▲ Steam rises from the dramatic sulphur springs at Soufrière.

LAND USE

Bananas

Bananas/other crops

Forest

Built-up areas

▲ Hotels

🏭 Factories

Climate and Weather

Most people think of St Lucia as a tropical island, where the sun shines all the time. But the island actually has more rainfall than Britain. Rains fall throughout the year, with the wettest season between June and November. It rains in short, heavy downpours, creating rushing streams of water. Heavy rainfall can damage roads, wash away precious topsoil and flood areas close to rivers. But the sun soon comes out again and quickly dries everything out. With heavy rainfall and high temperatures, it can feel very humid and sticky on the island.

A short, heavy downpour ▶ clears the air. It is wise to take your umbrella whenever you go out.

Temperature

The temperature in St Lucia is about 27–28 °C all year round. The strongest winds come from the north-east. These winds keep the east coast of the island slightly cooler than the west coast. The temperatures are much cooler in the mountains.

▼ St Lucia's high rainfall and hot weather provide the ideal climate for growing coconuts. This man is selling some from the back of his truck.

RAINY DAYS IN CASTRIES

| January – March: | 11 days a month |
| June – December: | 18 days a month |

ANNUAL RAINFALL

Castries:	2,000 mm
On the coast:	1,500 mm
In the mountains:	3,450 mm

Hurricanes

Every few years, St Lucia is struck by a severe hurricane or tropical storm. Hurricanes are given the names of girls one year, and boys the next. On 10 September 1994, Tropical Storm Debbie struck St Lucia, wreaking havoc. Extremely strong winds blowing at more than 70 kilometres an hour, destroyed houses, trees, and banana crops. Very heavy rain causes mudslides which can bury homes, and flooding, which cuts off villages. Usually a warning is given over the radio and people are kept up to date with what is happening. Even so, four people died during Tropical Storm Debbie, when landslides covered their homes as they slept.

Hurricane Lenny struck in 1999. It was different from other storms in that it approached from the west and seriously affected the holiday resorts along the coast.

▼ **Heavy rain has eroded the sides of this hill.**

Tropical Storm Debbie

'I was awakened by the sound of thunder and the lightning flashing brightly across my room. I was able to fall asleep again, listening to the sound of the rain tapping on the roof. In the morning, I saw that the yard was flooded. My big black and brown dog was in his kennel cleaning himself because he got wet in the rain.

'I looked up at the sky and saw big, thick, grey clouds. The streets were flooded with dirty water and garbage moving as quickly as a river. I put on the radio to hear the news. Schools were damaged, and roads were blocked by landslides, broken bridges and fallen trees.

'In spite of it all, everyone was determined to bring things back to normal. We all worked together. Within one week, our school was re-opened.'

▲ Eleven-year-old Shakima St Clair describes her own experience of Tropical Storm Debbie.

▶ Rebuilding houses after hurricanes and tropical storms costs the government a lot of money.

13

Plants and Animals

St Lucia's landscape ranges from dense rain forest to coastal waters. These varied habitats provide homes for all sorts of wildlife. The countryside is filled with the smell of flowers and the song of birds.

Rainforest Habitat

The rain forest is the perfect habitat for trees, such as teak and mahogany. These trees are called hardwoods, and they take many hundreds of years to grow. Their wood is very valuable and in the past was used to make high-quality furniture. But now St Lucians are trying to protect these trees because they take so long to grow.

Other plants, such as giant tree ferns, creepers and mosses, grow in shady areas of the rain forest. Beautiful, exotic flowers, such as orchids and hibiscus, bloom here all year round.

Ferns and mosses thrive ▶ in the thick rainforest undergrowth.

▼ The people in this workshop are making furniture from locally grown wood.

▲ A St Lucian parrot perches on a branch.

CASE STUDY

The Jacquot

The St Lucian parrot, nicknamed the 'Jacquot' is found only in St Lucia. This brightly coloured bird has recently come close to becoming extinct and is now a protected species. For many St Lucians, the Jacquot has become a symbol of conservation on the island. Special campaigns to educate the public and schoolchildren about the importance of conserving the environment are based around the Jacquot.

The rain forest also provides an excellent habitat for a great variety of animals and birds. Boa constrictors and smaller, but equally dangerous snakes slither along the forest floor. The branches of trees teem with tree frogs and humming birds. The rain forest is also home to the St Lucian parrot, one of the rarest birds in the world. As the rain forest is cut down, many of these animals are in danger of losing their homes.

Coastal Habitats

On the drier coastal plains, cacti and succulents can be found. In some areas, thick mangroves grow along the shoreline, at the water's edge. The mangroves protect the coast from erosion in strong storms.

A wide range of tropical fish and sea life can be found among the coral reefs, further out to sea. Coral reefs can be easily damaged by careless divers and people doing water sports. Turtles also swim in St Lucia's waters, but they are becoming increasingly rare.

Mangroves grow in the ▶ shallow waters around the coast.

▼ Tropical fish thrive in the coral reefs.

17

Settlements

Over 160,000 people live in various types of settlement in St Lucia. The island has one city, three towns and six main villages. Each of these settlements is the centre for an administrative district, or parish. There are also many smaller villages on the island.

▼ **Large cruise ships dock in Castries harbour.**

Castries

Castries is the capital city of St Lucia. It grew up as a port, and even today much of the city's life is based around the harbour. Most of the shops are found in the business district, close to the dockside. This area was rebuilt in 1948 after a major fire, so the buildings here are modern. The streets bustle with tourists buying gifts in the smart shops, and street traders selling a wide range of goods.

▼ Castries Harbour and its surroundings.

▲ Traffic and parking are some of the problems that nearly all towns on the island share.

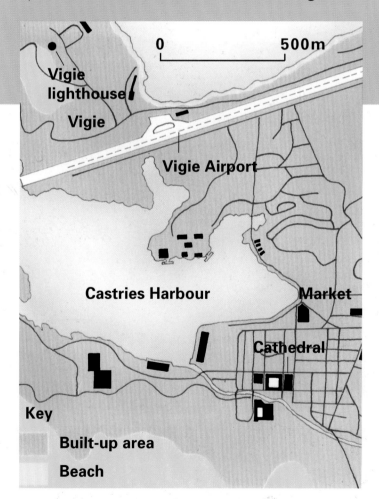

Key

Built-up area

Beach

Towards the centre of the island, the land rises quite steeply and is difficult to build on. Most settlements in St Lucia are found along the coast and at the mouths of rivers, where the land is fairly flat. You can see this if you look at a map and find the capital, Castries, and the three main towns of Vieux Fort, Soufrière and Gros Islet. Castries is built round a natural deep-water harbour which is able to take up to five large cruise ships at any one time. St Lucia's bananas are exported through the port here.

POPULATIONS OF MAJOR SETTLEMENTS

Castries:	62,967
Vieux Fort:	14,561
Gros Islet:	19,409
Soufrière:	7,337

▲ Vieux Fort is one of the few areas of flat land on the island. This area will probably soon be developed and built on.

St Lucia's Towns

St Lucia's three towns are Gros Islet, Vieux Fort and Soufrière. In the past, the main occupation in these towns was fishing. Today, although fishing still takes place, these towns are now the centres of St Lucia's booming tourist industry.

Vieux Fort is the second-largest town on the island and is built on a river delta. The town has several foreign-owned factories and most of the goods produced here are exported through Vieux Fort's own port.

Vieux Fort also has an airport, Hewanorra. All the international visitors arrive at Hewanorra airport. There is also an airport near Castries, at Vigie, which serves visitors from other islands in the Caribbean.

Key

— **Roads**

✈ **Airports**

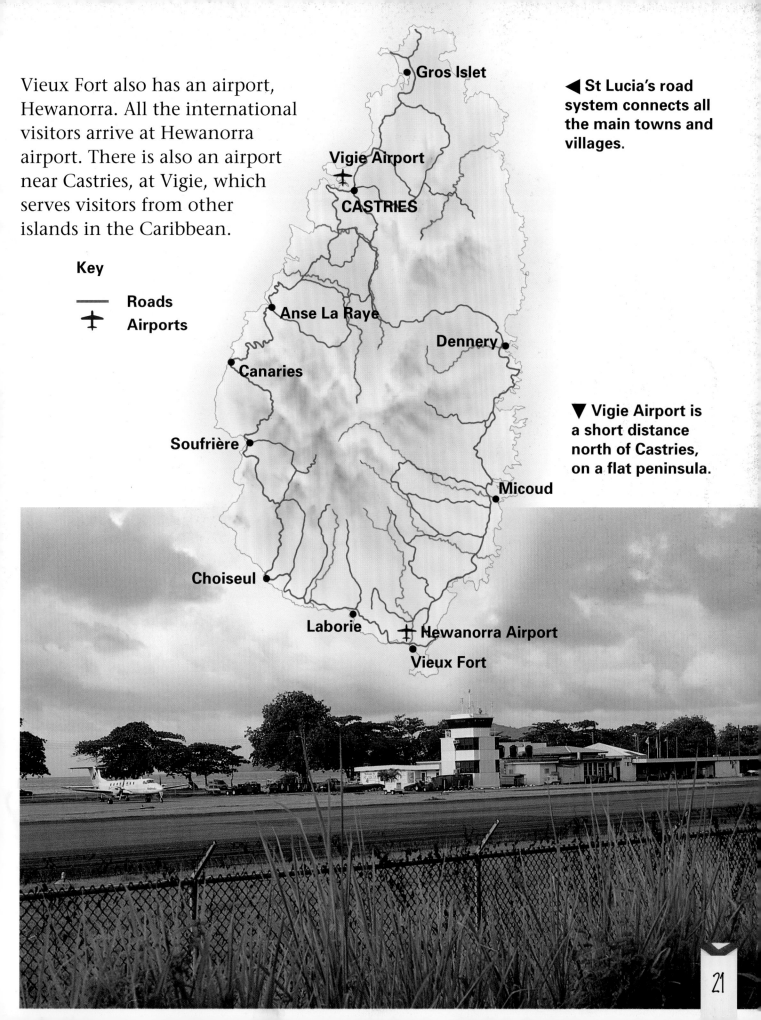

Gros Islet

Vigie Airport

CASTRIES

Anse La Raye

Dennery

Canaries

Soufrière

Micoud

Choiseul

Laborie   Hewanorra Airport

Vieux Fort

◄ **St Lucia's road system connects all the main towns and villages.**

▼ **Vigie Airport is a short distance north of Castries, on a flat peninsula.**

Villages

The six main villages of St Lucia are Laborie, Choiseul, Canaries, Dennery, Micoud and Anse la Raye. These settlements are on the coast and began as fishing villages. There are many smaller villages inland and further up the valleys. People who live here are farmers and usually grow bananas. These small villages are remote and often difficult to get to, with no proper road.

▼ Children from outlying farms and villages may have a long journey to school.

◀ Anse la Raye is a large village on St Lucia's west coast.

▼ Anse la Raye lies just between Castries and Canaries.

Anse la Raye

The name 'Anse la Raye' means 'The Bay of Rays' and the village is named after the stingrays that can be found in the sea here. Anse la Raye was once a fishing village. But now, the seas have been over-fished and fewer people are able to earn their living in this way. Anse la Raye is only 10 kilometres south of Castries, so many people from the village now commute there for work. The village has a population of just over 3,000 people.

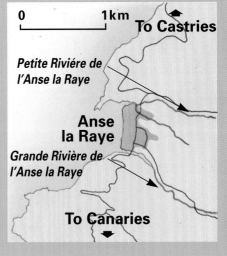

The West Coast

The best beaches in St Lucia are on the west coast. This is where most of the hotels and holiday resorts are found. New hotels are being built all the time. Work is being done to improve the roads in St Lucia so that it is easier to travel from one place to another. Not so long ago people had to travel by boat to reach some places because there was no road.

◀ A road winds its way through the inland forest.

Natural Resources

St Lucia's rich landscape provides a variety of natural resources, which help the island to earn its living. The island's main resources are bananas, and its beautiful scenery and good climate.

Bananas

Bananas are grown on 85 per cent of the land available for farming in St Lucia. More than half of the people who work on the island are involved in some way in the banana industry. They grow them, clean them, pack them, transport them or load them on to ships.

▼ Fishing boats setting out to sea. Fishing is the traditional industry in many coastal villages.

▲ **The Cul de Sac banana plantation covers many kilometres.**

St Lucia has the largest banana crop in the Windward Islands. But it is always risky for a farmer or a country to rely on just one crop. A hurricane could wipe out the entire crop in one night and there would be little else for the islanders to rely on to bring in money. Small farmers are now being encouraged to grow a range of different crops so they are not so dependent on bananas. A growing demand from the tourist hotels for exotic fruit and vegetables also means that farmers are having to grow other crops.

◀ **Bananas and plantains for sale in Castries market.**

Tourism

In 2003, 342,000 visitors came to spend their holidays in St Lucia. This number is going up every year. Most tourists come from the USA, Britain and other Caribbean islands. It is not only the beautiful beaches that attract people but also the lush rain forest and the volcano. The number of people who visit St Lucia each year is more than three times the number of people who actually live here. Unfortunately, many tourists stay on their cruise ships or in foreign-owned hotels and they do not buy goods from local people. Some of the more expensive hotels fence off beaches. This means that local people cannot use them.

Giant palm trees tower ▶ over many of St Lucia's sandy beaches.

CASE STUDY

Hotel Worker

Carlton Newton is twenty years old. He works in the Hotel Seraphine, just north of Castries harbour. The hotel has twenty rooms, with a swimming pool overlooking the sea. Carlton manages the reception area of the hotel. Like many of the other workers at the hotel, he works in shifts. This can be hard work, especially during the peak season.

'I love St Lucia! It's a paradise. Working in the tourist industry gives me a chance to show off my country,' says Carlton.

◀ A view of Hotel Seraphine, on St Lucia's west coast.

VISITORS TO ST LUCIA

Origin	Numbers
USA	75,000
Caribbean	60,000
UK	51,000
Germany	13,000
Rest of Europe	21,000
Rest of the World	4,000

A Changing Environment

St Lucia is a small island that needs to make a living. The tourist industry provides jobs for people, but at the same time puts a lot of pressure on the environment. An increase in tourists means that there is a growing need for more hotels to accommodate them. There is not much flat land in St Lucia on which hotels can be built. They are often built in areas that are especially beautiful. The land has to be cleared, destroying fragile habitats and wildlife.

Producing Food

Farming puts a lot of pressure on the land. To grow more bananas, farmers use pesticides, which are bad for the environment. Over-fishing, not just by St Lucians but also by people from other islands, is another serious problem. The fish stocks are quickly running out.

▼ Many homes now have solar panels, storing energy from the Sun to make electricity.

Jacquot Comic

St Lucians are taking environmental issues very seriously. The Forestry Department has produced a comic named after the Jacquot to help with their education programme. The comic is filled with games, stories, cartoons and advice, to make St Lucia's children aware of their environment.

'The comic is great for children because it is fun, with colour pictures and cartoons,' says Ian Celestin, aged twelve.

Ian Celestin leafs through the ▶ Jacquot comic.

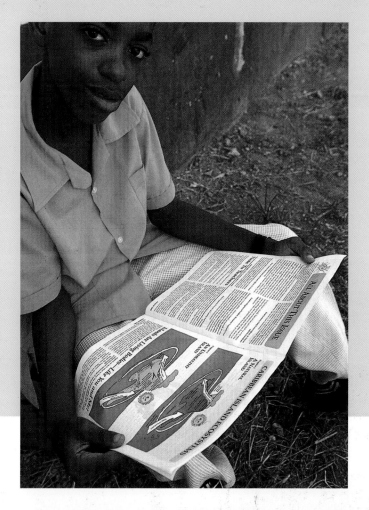

Caring for the Environment

People in St Lucia have realized that if they do not do something their island could be spoilt for ever. Environmental groups in St Lucia and ordinary members of the public are taking action to preserve their beautiful and unique island.

A bus visits villages giving ▶ people information on how to protect wildlife.

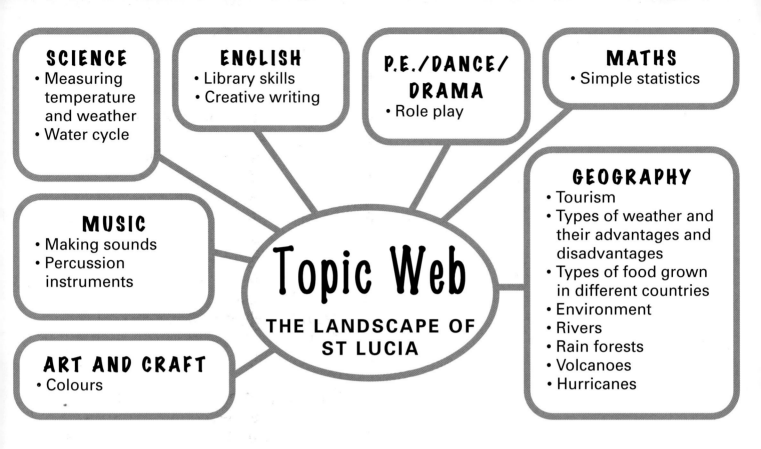

SCIENCE
• Measuring temperature and weather
• Water cycle

ENGLISH
• Library skills
• Creative writing

P.E./DANCE/ DRAMA
• Role play

MATHS
• Simple statistics

MUSIC
• Making sounds
• Percussion instruments

ART AND CRAFT
• Colours

Topic Web
THE LANDSCAPE OF ST LUCIA

GEOGRAPHY
• Tourism
• Types of weather and their advantages and disadvantages
• Types of food grown in different countries
• Environment
• Rivers
• Rain forests
• Volcanoes
• Hurricanes

Extension Activities

GEOGRAPHY
• Using atlases and globes, find St Lucia's exact location in relation other islands in the Caribbean.
• Think about the environmental issues that affect the place where you live. Create your own environmental comic to make your friends aware of what they can do to look after their environment.

DESIGN AND TECHNOLOGY
• Design a holiday brochure for St Lucia.
• Design a simple rain gauge to measure rainfall in your area.
• Investigate how to build a hurricane-proof house.

ENGLISH
• Make a list of new words you have come across in this book. Look up their meaning in the glossary or in a dictionary.
• Read *My Grandpa and the Sea* to find out more about the life of a traditional fisherman in St Lucia.
• Write a postcard to a friend telling them what there is to see in St Lucia.
• Write a newspaper article about Tropical Storm Debbie.

SCIENCE
• Investigate the special features of plants that grow in hot and humid environments.
• Find out why St Lucia has approximately 12 hours of light and 12 hours of dark all year round.
• Find out what would happen if the rain forest in St Lucia was all cut down.

P.E./DANCE/DRAMA
• Make up a role play entitled 'The Night of the Hurricane'.

MUSIC
• Using percussion instruments, try to create the sounds of the rain forest.

MATHS/INFORMATION TECHNOLOGY
• Make graphs or pie charts from the statistics in the fact boxes in this book.
• Produce some of these graphs or pie charts using computer software.
• Work out what percentage of days it rains in St Lucia.

ART AND CRAFT
• Paint a colourful rainforest frieze for your classroom wall.

Glossary

Administrative district An area of a country that has it's own local government.

Business district The central area of a town or city where the offices and shops are located.

Irrigation To water land using a series of canals.

Delta A triangular piece of earth, deposited by a river where it meets the sea.

Erosion The wearing away of rocks and soil caused by the action of water, wind, and ice.

Habitats The place where any living thing can be found.

Hardwoods Trees whose timber is especially hard and strong.

Mangroves A kind of shrub found in the muddy swamps of tropical coasts.

Peninsula A piece of land that juts out into the sea, and is almost completely surrounded by water.

Pesticides Any chemical used in farming to destroy animal pests.

Ravines Deep, narrow gorges.

Resources Supplies of natural materials.

Sulphur A yellow substance with an unpleasant smell, found in the craters of volcanoes.

Topsoil The upper layer of soil in which plants grow.

Volcanic plug A volcanic plug is the hard centre of a volcano that is sometimes all that is left after millions of years of erosion.

Further Information

Non-fiction:
The People of St Lucia by Alison Brownlie (Hodder Wayland, 2001)
Living in St Lucia Pupil's Book by Vincent Bunce and Wendy Morgan (Cambridge University Press, 1996) Also available to complement this title are a teacher's resource book, and a set of twelve A3 photocards.

Fiction:
My Grandpa and the Sea by Katherine Orr (Sagebrush Education Resources, 1991)

Photopacks:
Focus on Castries, St Lucia by Vincent Bunce, James Foley, Wendy Morgan and Steve Scoble (Geographical Association/Worldaware, 1997).
Go Bananas A photo-based activity pack focusing on the journey of a banana (Oxfam, 2000).

Visual resources:
Hello St Lucia! Hello England! 30 minute video available from Worldaware (Suffolk County Council, 2002)

Useful addresses:
For school links with St Lucia contact:
The Ministry of Education and Culture (Primary), Castries, St Lucia, West Indies.
Oxfam (Education), 274 Banbury Road, Oxford OX2 7DZ. Tel: 01865 311311.
The St Lucia Tourist Board, 1 Collingham Gardens, London SW5 0HW. Tel: 0870 900 7697
Worldaware, 42 High Street, Croydon CR0 1YB. Tel: 020 8686 8667

Index